BEGINNING TO END

Bulb to Tulip

by Rachel Grack

BELLWETHER MEDIA • MINNEAPOLIS, MN

Note to Librarians, Teachers, and Parents:

Blastoff! Readers are carefully developed by literacy experts and combine standards-based content with developmentally appropriate text.

Level 1 provides the most support through repetition of high-frequency words, light text, predictable sentence patterns, and strong visual support.

Level 2 offers early readers a bit more challenge through varied simple sentences, increased text load, and less repetition of high-frequency words.

Level 3 advances early-fluent readers toward fluency through increased text and concept load, less reliance on visuals, longer sentences, and more literary language.

Level 4 builds reading stamina by providing more text per page, increased use of punctuation, greater variation in sentence patterns, and increasingly challenging vocabulary.

Level 5 encourages children to move from "learning to read" to "reading to learn" by providing even more text, varied writing styles, and less familiar topics.

Whichever book is right for your reader, Blastoff! Readers are the perfect books to build confidence and encourage a love of reading that will last a lifetime!

This edition first published in 2020 by Bellwether Media, Inc.

No part of this publication may be reproduced in whole or in part without written permission of the publisher. For information regarding permission, write to Bellwether Media, Inc., Attention: Permissions Department, 6012 Blue Circle Drive, Minnetonka, MN 55343.

Library of Congress Cataloging-in-Publication Data

Names: Koestler-Grack, Rachel A., 1973- author.
Title: Bulb to Tulip / by Rachel Grack.
Description: Minneapolis, MN : Bellwether Media, Inc., [2020] | Series: Blastoff! readers: Beginning to end | Includes bibliographical references and index. | Audience: Ages 5-8 | Audience: Grades K-1 |
Summary: "Relevant images match informative text in this introduction to how tulips grow. Intended for students in kindergarten through third grade"– Provided by publisher.
Identifiers: LCCN 2019026689 (print) | LCCN 2019026690 (ebook) |
ISBN 9781644871379 (library binding) | ISBN 9781618918079 (ebook)
Subjects: LCSH: Tulips–Juvenile literature. | Bulbs (Plants)–Juvenile literature.
Classification: LCC SB413.T9 G69 2020 (print) | LCC SB413.T9 (ebook) | DDC 635.9/3469–dc23
LC record available at https://lccn.loc.gov/2019026689
LC ebook record available at https://lccn.loc.gov/2019026690

Editor: Rebecca Sabelko   Designer: Laura Sowers

Printed in the United States of America, North Mankato, MN.

Table of Contents

Bulb Beginnings

bulb

Did you know tulips grow from bulbs?

Where Do Tulips Grow?

N
W E
S

The Netherlands produces over 3 billion tulips each year.

Bulbs begin as seeds. Each bulb grows more bulbs. They take years to **bloom**!

Growing Cycle

seed pod

Pollination produces seed pods in tulip flowers. The pods dry out and crack open.

Seeds spread on the ground. They **germinate** and take root.

tulip seeds germinating

Seedlings come up in spring.
They only grow leaves.
They do not flower for the
first four years.

Soon bulbs begin to form.

Each year, bulbs grow layers of thick **leaf scales**. These store **nutrients** and water.

They help the plant form. A papery **tunic** covers them.

leaf scales

Traveling Flowers

8 out of 10 cut flowers grown in Latin America are sold in the United States

tunic

basal plate and roots

Roots grow from the **basal plate**. They pull nutrients from the soil.

A tulip bud, stem, and leaves
form inside the bulb. It can now
be dug up!

Flowers Form

People plant bulbs in fall.
The bulbs rest through the winter.

What Makes a Tulip Grow?

soil

water

sunlight

nutrients stored in the leaf scales

Spring sunshine warms the soil.
The plant pushes out of the bulb.
Up comes a tulip flower!

Tulips bloom in May or June.
They come in a rainbow of colors.

The flowers last up to
two weeks before they **wilt**.

wilted tulips

17

bulblets

Then the bulb starts multiplying. **Bulblets** grow from the basal plate. They feed off the mother bulb. Soon they are fully formed. The cycle begins again!

Life Cycle of a Tulip

pollination

flowers and
bulblets form

germination

bulbs make buds

bulbs form and
seedlings grow

Bringing Smiles

Tulips are among the first flowers to bloom in spring.

These colorful flowers make a great Mother's Day gift. They bring many smiles!

Glossary

basal plate—the flat bottom of a bulb; roots grow from the basal plate.

bloom—to make flowers; flowers are in bloom when they open.

bulblets—baby bulbs that grow off of a mother bulb

germinate—to sprout and grow roots

leaf scales—soft, thick layers in a bulb that become leaves; leaf scales provide food and water to the bulb.

nutrients—the food plants need to grow

pollination—the movement of pollen from one flower to another; pollen is a yellow dust that is needed to produce seeds.

seedlings—young plants

tunic—the papery coating that covers the leaf scales of a bulb

wilt—to droop and start to die

To Learn More

AT THE LIBRARY

Levy, Janey. *How Plants Spread Seeds*. New York, N.Y.: Gareth Stevens Publishing, 2020.

Owings, Lisa. *From Bulb to Tulip*. Minneapolis, Minn.: Lerner Publications, 2015.

Whipple, Annette. *Flowers*. Vero Beach, Fla.: Rourke Educational Media, 2017.

ON THE WEB

FACTSURFER

Factsurfer.com gives you a safe, fun way to find more information.

1. Go to www.factsurfer.com.

2. Enter "bulb to tulip" into the search box and click Q.

3. Select your book cover to see a list of related web sites.

Index

The images in this book are reproduced through the courtesy of: GrahamIrvin, front cover (tulips); eXpose, front cover (bulbs); Tommy Atthi, p. 3; OlgaPonomarenko, pp. 4-5; Denis Pogostin, pp. 6-7, 19 (1); IgorPloskin, pp. 7, 19 (2); lesichkadesign, pp. 8-9; TanaCh, p. 9; Kazakov Maksim, pp. 10, 15 (leaf scales); Lumikk555, pp. 10-11; ronstik, p. 12 (bulb); grafvision, p. 12 (soil); Sarycheva Olesia, pp. 11-12; inomasa, pp. 14-15; bluedog studio, p. 14 (soil); RG-vc, p. 14 (water); Nataliia K, p. 14 (sunlight); Olena Z, pp. 16-17; gipi23, p. 17; Oksix, pp. 18, 19 (5); cla78, p. 19 (3); dms.spb, p. 19 (4); Yuganov Konstantin, pp. 20-21; Sisika, p. 21.